W

*"I think I'm the first man to sit
on the top of the world."*

— Matthew Henson

MATTHEW HENSON AND THE NORTH POLE EXPEDITION

By Ann Graham Gaines

The Child's World®

GRAPHIC DESIGN
Robert E. Bonaker / Graphic Design & Consulting Co.

PROJECT COORDINATOR
James R. Rothaus / James R. Rothaus & Associates

EDITORIAL DIRECTION
Elizabeth Sirimarco Budd

COVER PHOTO
Portrait of Matthew Henson
©Bettmann/CORBIS

The editor would like to thank Verne Robinson (www.matthewhenson.com)
for his helpful advice and for supplying many of the photographs.

Library of Congress Cataloging-in-Publication Data
Gaines, Ann.
Matthew Henson and the North Pole expedition / by Ann Graham Gaines.
p. cm.
Includes bibliographical references.
Summary: A brief biography of the black explorer and
seaman who, together with Robert E. Peary,
discovered the North Pole in 1909.
ISBN 1-56766-743-0 (lib. reinforced : alk. paper)

1.Henson, Matthew Alexander, 1866–1955 — Juvenile literature. 2. Afro-
American explorers — Biography — Juvenile literature. 3. North Pole —
Discovery and exploration — Juvenile literature. [1. Henson, Matthew
Alexander, 1866–1955. 2. Explorers. 3. Afro-Americans — Biography.
4. North Pole] I. Title

G635.H4 G35 2000
919.8 — dc21   99-047519
[B]

Contents

April 6, 1909   6

Young Matt Henson   12

Early Adventures   18

To the North Pole!   25

After the Pole   33

Timeline   36

Glossary   37

Index   39

Further Information   40

April 6, 1909

In 1909, African American Matthew Henson took part in a great adventure. He went along on an **expedition,** led by explorer Robert Peary, to the North Pole.

For years, Peary had dreamed of becoming the first person ever to reach the Pole. He and Henson had already failed to get there once. Peary believed he had one last chance to explore the Arctic. At nearly 53 years old, he no longer felt as strong as he once did. He knew he must plan his expedition carefully.

Peary found a group of brave, smart men to go with him. He explained what they could expect of the journey. They would have to leave solid land and cross the ice-covered Arctic Ocean. They would travel so far north that they would meet no other humans. There would be no villages where they could stop for rest or supplies. They would have to make camps on their way. There would be no animals to hunt. Everything they needed they would have to carry with them. The journey would test their courage and their strength.

Peary's expedition left their camp on Ellesmere Island, north of Canada in the Arctic Ocean, on March 1, 1909. Peary had six **assistants.** Matthew Henson was one of them. Each assistant led a team of three **Inuit** men. Traveling on dog **sledges,** they took turns cutting a trail and moving supplies ahead. From the start, Peary planned to take just one team all the way to the Pole. As the troop grew closer to its goal, Peary sent the teams back, one by one. Fewer people meant he needed fewer supplies. As they headed south, the returning teams also kept the trail open. The open trail would help Peary find his way back. Otherwise, wind and ice would erase their tracks.

Courtesy of Verne Robinson

MATTHEW HENSON WAS A VITAL MEMBER OF THE FIRST EXPEDITION TO REACH THE NORTH POLE.

Courtesy of Verne Robinson

To travel across the frozen Arctic Ocean, the Peary expedition depended on sledges pulled by strong, healthy dogs.

On March 31, 1909, Peary decided which team would go all the way to the North Pole. He made the last leg of his journey with just five other men: Matthew Henson and four Inuit named Egingwah, Seegloo, Ootah, and Ooqueah. Peary had a good reason to choose Henson to make the hardest part of the journey. He had the most arctic experience of all Peary's assistants. He spoke the Inuit language better than the others. And he was very good at sledge driving and dog handling.

For five days, Peary, Henson, and the others struggled across the ice. They pushed their bodies to the limit. They traveled for 10 hours at a time. Along the way, Henson and the Inuit built igloos where they could sleep. To keep from freezing, they made tea over portable stoves. All they had to eat was **pemmican** and hard **ship biscuits.**

The team also grew thirsty because they did not have enough water to drink. For the little water they had, the men melted snow, using the portable stoves. They faced terrible cold. Henson often had to help the dogs by pushing the sledges over jagged piles of ice. Every morning, Peary would first start off on foot and cover a few miles. Henson soon caught up on his dog sledge. For the rest of the day, Peary then rode on a sledge driven by one of the Inuit. He was not as strong as he once had been. In fact, he had suffered **frostbite** many years before and had lost eight of his toes. Henson went ahead of the team, finding the way.

On April 3, Henson experienced a terrible scare. As he crossed moving ice, he fell into frigid water. He was lucky. Ootah reached him and grabbed him by the back of his neck. Ootah had saved Henson's life. Henson would have done the same for any member of their group.

Finally, on April 6, Matthew Henson was out ahead of the group. He reached a point he thought was the North Pole. There he built an igloo. Peary arrived on a sledge about 45 minutes later. Henson greeted him, saying, "I think I'm the first man to sit on the top of the world."

Peary was furious that Henson had beaten him. He was so mad that he did not speak to Henson for the rest of the trip, except to give him orders. But Peary could not tell for sure whether they had really reached the North Pole. To do so, he had to use a **sextant.** This special tool could tell exactly where the sun was in the sky. Peary could use it to determine the group's location. At first, there were too many clouds to use the sextant. Peary raised his flag and ordered the group to rest.

While Henson and the others slept, the sun broke through the clouds. Peary used his sextant. He decided the team remained three miles short of their goal. Soon he set off — without telling Henson — for what he thought must be the Pole. One day later, he led the entire party to that spot — just 150 yards from where Henson had been! When they arrived, they raised flags and posed for photographs. Then they loaded up their sledges and prepared to travel 500 miles back to their ship, the *Roosevelt*.

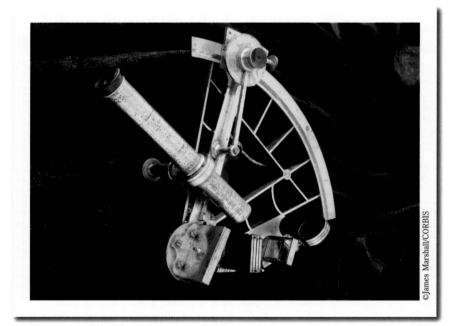
©James Marshall/CORBIS

A SEXTANT WAS A VERY IMPORTANT TOOL FOR EXPLORERS. IT HELPED THEM DETERMINE EXACTLY WHERE THEY WERE AND TO FIND THEIR WAY HOME.

Courtesy of Verne Robinson

WHEN PEARY'S TEAM REACHED THE NORTH POLE, THEY DID NOT STAY VERY LONG. THEY KNEW THE TRIP BACK TO THEIR SHIP WOULD BE A DIFFICULT ONE.

Young Matt Henson

The Northern states had just won the **American Civil War** when Matthew Alexander Henson was born on August 8, 1866. The Henson family lived in Charles County, Maryland. Slavery was legal in Maryland until 1865. That year, the 13th **Amendment** ended slavery everywhere in the United States. Matthew's parents were different from most other African Americans who lived in Maryland at the time because they had been born free.

Matthew's mother died when he was just two years old. His father remarried soon after. His new wife, Nellie, was a cruel woman. She beat Matthew and his brothers and sisters. Unfortunately, Matthew's father died a few years after he married Nellie. She became even more angry and violent. One day, just after Matthew's 11th birthday, she beat him very badly. He spent three days in bed. Matthew knew he had to leave.

In the dark of night, Matthew ran away from home. He ended up in the city of Washington, D.C. For a while, he washed dishes in a restaurant. The restaurant's owner was a friendly, gentle woman named Janey. She let Matthew live with her. She felt sorry that she could not afford to send him to school.

One day, a man who claimed to have sailed around the world came to the restaurant. He told wonderful stories. Matthew knew right then that he wanted to be a sailor and see the world, too. A few days later, he said good-bye to Janey. He walked about 50 miles to Baltimore, Maryland.

Courtesy of Verne Robinson

MATTHEW HENSON WAS BORN ON AUGUST 8, 1866, IN MARYLAND.

Baltimore was an important port. Matthew hoped he could find work on a ship. On the docks, he met a kind old man named Captain Childs. They began to talk. Captain Childs owned a ship. He sailed all over the world, stopping at ports to buy and sell goods. He liked Matthew and wanted to help him. He told Matthew he could go along as a **cabin boy** on his next voyage. Before he knew it, Matthew was on his way to China!

Matthew worked for Captain Childs for four years. After just one voyage, he had become, as Matthew later said, "an able-bodied seaman." He could hoist sails, tie knots, and read charts. Childs also had taught him geography and history. Together they read the Bible. By the time he was 17 years old, Matthew had traveled to Japan, Taiwan, North Africa, Spain, France, and Russia.

In 1884, Captain Childs died while on a voyage. After his ship returned to port, Henson no longer went to sea — but no one really knows why. Perhaps he thought he might not have been able to find another ship's captain who would treat an African American worker as well as Captain Childs did.

For the next two years, Henson took whatever work he could find. In 1886, at age 20, he moved back to Washington. There, he lived with his sister and her family. He took a job as a clerk at Steinmetz & Sons, a clothing store. One day in 1887, Robert Peary came in to the shop. Peary was a U.S. Navy **engineer.** He had just returned from a trip to the island of Greenland.

At that time, people were very interested in what they called the "Greenland problem." Northeast Greenland did not appear on maps because it had not yet been explored. Peary had gone there because he wanted to be the one who discovered the exact shape of the island. The puzzle **intrigued** him. He also wanted to become famous. Exploring Greenland could win him glory. One day, he also hoped to explore the polar ice cap, a huge area of ice that sits on top of the Arctic Ocean. In most places, the polar ice cap is so thick and strong that animals, including humans and polar bears, can walk on it.

©Peter Harholdt/CORBIS

WHEN YOUNG MATTHEW HEARD A MAN TELL STORIES OF LIFE AT SEA, HE LONGED TO BECOME A SAILOR. HE DREAMED OF TRAVELING THE WORLD ON A SHIP. HIS DREAM CAME TRUE WHEN HE MET CAPTAIN CHILDS. HENSON LEFT BALTIMORE TO SAIL THE WORLD.

Courtesy of Verne Robinson

TODAY ROBERT PEARY IS HONORED AS THE
FIRST EXPLORER TO REACH THE NORTH POLE.
HENSON FIRST MET PEARY IN 1887.

The U.S. Navy had asked Peary to make a map of Nicaragua, a small country in Central America. Nicaragua is part of the **isthmus** between North and South America. This separates the Atlantic Ocean from the Pacific Ocean. Navy officials hoped Peary would find a good **canal** route for ships to pass through the isthmus. Today vessels travel through the Panama Canal to accomplish this, but in Peary's time, the canal had not yet been built.

Peary heard Henson talk about the time he had spent sailing the globe. He asked Henson to come along as his **valet.** Henson later wrote that he did not want to become a servant. But Peary was an unusual man. "I recognized in him the qualities that made me willing to engage myself in his service," wrote Henson. He believed Peary would treat him fairly. Also, he wanted to see Central America. Peary would give him this chance.

THE NARROW ISTHMUS BETWEEN NORTH AND SOUTH AMERICA SEPARATES THE ATLANTIC AND PACIFIC OCEANS. UNTIL THE PANAMA CANAL WAS BUILT, SHIPS HAD TO SAIL ALL THE WAY AROUND SOUTH AMERICA TO GET FROM ONE OCEAN TO THE OTHER. THE U.S. NAVY SENT PEARY TO CENTRAL AMERICA, HOPING HE WOULD FIND AN IDEAL ROUTE TO BUILD A CANAL.

NORTH AMERICA

ATLANTIC OCEAN

ISTHMUS OF PANAMA

SOUTH AMERICA

PACIFIC OCEAN

ANTARCTICA

Early Adventures

In the steamy jungles of Nicaragua, Henson did much more than the usual valet's duties. He also acted as a mechanic, carpenter, and **navigator.** Peary also asked him to help make maps. They returned to the United States in the summer of 1888. Peary remained in the navy, and Henson went back to work at the Steinmetz store.

One year later, Peary helped Henson get a job as a messenger at the League Island Navy Yard in Philadelphia. Peary had moved to that city after he married a woman named Josephine Diebitsch. Henson decided to take the job. At the time, many blacks led comfortable lives in Philadelphia. They could earn good pay working as carpenters, builders, and blacksmiths. For a time, Henson felt like an outsider in the new city. After joining a church, he began to make friends. He met a young woman named Eva Helen Flint. Soon they talked of marriage.

In February of 1891, Peary asked Henson to come see him at his office. He told Henson that the navy had agreed to give him time off for his exploring expedition to Greenland. Peary asked Henson to come along as his personal assistant. Henson would have to quit his job to make the journey. Eva did not like this. But Henson told her he hoped the trip would gain fame for both Peary and himself. Then Peary could find him more work in the future. It was a difficult decision, but Henson accepted Peary's offer. Eva agreed with his plan. On April 16, 1891, Henson and Eva married.

In June, Peary began his second trip to Greenland. Six other men and Peary's wife, Josephine, went with him and Henson. On board their ship, the *Kite*, Henson organized the team's supplies.

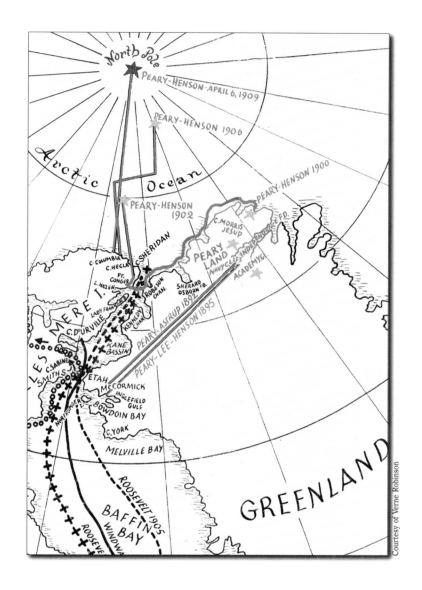

North Pole

PEARY-HENSON · APRIL 6, 1909

PEARY-HENSON 1906

PEARY-HENSON 1900

Arctic *Ocean*

PEARY-HENSON 1902

C. MORRIS JESUP

PEARY LAND

C. SHERIDAN

C. COLUMBIA
C. HECLA
FT. CONGER
L. HAZEN

ROBESON CHAN.

SHERARD OSBORN FD.

NAVYCLIFF INDEPENDENCE FD.

ACADEMY G.

PEARY-ASTRUP 1892

PEARY-LEE-HENSON 1895

E L L E S M E R E I.

C. D'URVILLE

LADY FRANKLIN B.

KENNEDY CHAN.

KANE BASSIN

C. SABINE

SMITHS S.

ETAH
McCORMICK
INGLEFIELD GULF
BOWDOIN BAY

NORTHUMBERLAND IS.

C. YORK

MELVILLE BAY

ROOSEVELT 1905

BAFFIN BAY

WINDWARD

ROOSEVELT

GREENLAND

Courtesy of Verne Robinson

HENSON AND PEARY ACCOMPLISHED MANY GREAT EXPEDITIONS TOGETHER BEFORE THEY FINALLY MADE IT TO THE NORTH POLE IN 1909. THIS MAP SHOWS THE ROUTES AND FINAL DESTINATIONS FOR SIX OF THEIR TRIPS.

HENSON AND PEARY BUILT IGLOOS WHEN THEY TRAVELED ACROSS THE ARCTIC. THE INUIT TAUGHT HENSON TO CRAFT THESE SHELTERS MADE OF ICE AND SNOW.

On July 26, the group went ashore. Henson built a shelter where the group spent the winter. During this time, he began to meet Inuit. (Like others who traveled to the Arctic in those days, Henson and Peary called these **natives** Eskimos.) In the summer, the Inuit moved about, pitching tents wherever the hunting seemed best. In the winter, they lived in stone houses. They used igloos built of snow and ice for shelter on winter hunting trips. Henson made friends with the Inuit people. He learned to speak their language and taught them some English. The Inuit invited him to hunt with them. They showed him how to drive the dog sledges they used to travel over snow and ice. They showed Henson how to build igloos. They gave him warm clothing made of fur.

In the spring, Peary and his men set off to cross Greenland. Peary's wife stayed behind in the camp. The trip was very difficult. The team often faced terribly strong winds. Henson had to turn back because his heel was frostbitten. He was disappointed, but he still felt happy that he had made the journey to the Arctic.

This was the first of seven trips to the Arctic that Henson would take with Peary over the next 18 years. They came close to starving on their 1895 expedition. In 1898, they faced especially chilling cold. Frostbite caused Peary to lose eight toes. In 1901, they finally reached their goal to explore Greenland's farthest reaches. Henson called it a "long race with death." When they finally returned home, Henson vowed never to return to the Arctic again.

He changed his mind, however. Henson had learned to love life in the icy northern climate. Also, he usually got along well with Peary, and he liked adventure.

Peary made new plans. What he really wanted was to be the first man to reach the North Pole. Other explorers were also working toward this goal. To achieve it, Peary founded the Peary Arctic Club. The club raised money for him. People began to read about Peary in newspapers. When Peary made speeches, Henson went along to help him. He even wore Inuit clothing at such events.

By this time, Henson was single again. Eva grew tired of his leaving home for long periods of time. They divorced in 1897. Waiting for Peary to raise enough funds, Henson took different jobs. He worked as a **porter** for a while, and then as a janitor.

In 1905, Peary and Henson returned to the Arctic to make what they thought would be their trip to the North Pole. They made it farther north than any explorer had ever gone, but they had to turn back. The group reached a point where the polar ice cap had broken, revealing the frigid water that lay below. They could walk no farther. They also ran out of food. Both Peary and Henson were disappointed. By this point, Peary was 50. Henson was about to turn 40. They knew they would not always have the strength to make such trips.

On their voyage home, the men decided they would try to reach the North Pole once more the next year. By this time, Peary depended on Henson. A strong man, Henson worked well with his hands. He could make an igloo quickly. He built strong sledges, and he could fix them when something went wrong. Henson was a great outdoorsman, too. He hunted animals for food and for the furs that Inuit women sewed into clothing for them. Peary put him in charge of training the dogs that pulled their sledges. Henson even tried to get to know the people who lived in the Arctic. The Inuit liked Peary because he gave them things in exchange for helping him. But they saw Henson as a friend. The Inuit found him so friendly that they nicknamed him *Maripaluk,* or "kind Matthew."

Courtesy of Verne Robinson

THE INUIT WERE FOND OF HENSON. HE LEARNED THEIR LANGUAGE
AND WAS FRIENDLY TO THEM. THE INUIT WOMEN HELPED HIM BY
SEWING ANIMAL FURS INTO WARM CLOTHING. THE INUIT MEN
HELPED HIM BUILD SLEDGES AND TRAIN THE DOGS.

©Flip Schulke/CORBIS

THE *ROOSEVELT* TRANSPORTED PEARY'S TEAM NORTHWARD UP
THE ATLANTIC OCEAN TO ELLESMERE ISLAND.

To the North Pole!

When they got back to New York, Peary set to work raising money for the new expedition. Henson worked on their ship, the *Roosevelt*. He gathered supplies and equipment. He also married his second wife, Lucy Jane Ross.

Peary **recruited** five other assistants for the expedition. He also hired a ship's crew. Their trip began when they sailed from New York City on July 6, 1908. President Theodore Roosevelt came to the harbor to wish them well and say good-bye.

In the first week of August, the USS *Roosevelt* docked in Etah on the island of Greenland. Peary found Inuit families to travel with them. Altogether, 39 Inuit men, women, and children boarded the ship. They brought hundreds of dogs with them. Peary also bought coal and supplied the ship with meat from seals, walruses, and **narwhal** that Henson and the Inuit had hunted. Then they sailed north again.

Ice in the water made the journey slow and difficult. On September 5, 1908, the ship landed on Cape Sheridan, on Canada's Ellesmere Island. The explorers made a camp where they spent most of the next winter getting ready for their trip across the ice.

Henson left camp twice on hunting trips that lasted more than a week. Back at camp, he got the equipment and supplies ready. He built 24 sledges. He worked with the Inuit's dogs. He divided the dogs into teams and got them used to wearing a harness. During this period, Henson and the others went for three months without ever seeing the sun. (The sun never rises in the Arctic during the winter.) The temperature could dip to more than 50 or 60 degrees below zero. Sometimes the storms were so strong that winds carried huge boxes of supplies through the air. All winter long, Henson and other members of Peary's team drove dog sledges farther north, dropping supplies the expedition would use on its trip to the Pole.

On February 18, 1909, Henson and a group of Inuit left the *Roosevelt* for Cape Columbia, a point farther north on Ellesmere Island. When they woke up at 5:30 AM, the thermometer read –28 degrees. They were ready to go by 7:30. Their sledges carried pemmican, biscuits, tea, water, and the alcohol they needed to run their portable stoves. But suddenly, a terrible wind came up. They had to wait more than an hour to leave.

It took four days to get to Cape Columbia. When they arrived, they built what they called "Crane City," a camp with several large igloos. From Crane City, they would move supplies to Cape Aldrich. From Cape Aldrich, Peary planned to leave land and move out onto the frozen ice. Soon all the members of the expedition had arrived. For the first time in months, they could see a band of sunlight on the horizon at noon. Early in March, the sun would finally begin to rise.

On February 28, Peary sent team member Robert Bartlett out ahead of the others. He and three Inuit would make a trail for the others to follow. On March 1, Peary ordered the rest of the group to move out. Henson and three Inuit led the others.

Peary had calculated that they would have to travel 413 miles to reach the Pole. For the next month, each of Peary's teams took turns leading the way. The lead team created a trail and moved supplies forward for the rest of the group.

The trip across the frozen polar sea proved difficult. Sometimes they had to use axes to cut paths through piles of ice. Sledges broke down, and they had to stop and fix them. Henson would never forget the pain he felt when he had to remove his mittens in the biting cold to tighten the sledge straps.

WITH HELP FROM THE INUIT, HENSON BUILT THE 24 SLEDGES
USED ON THE EXPEDITION. THEY HAD TO BE VERY STURDY TO
TRAVEL ACROSS THE JAGGED ARCTIC ICE.

A LEAD IS A LONG CRACK IN THE ARCTIC ICE THAT EXPOSES THE OCEAN BELOW. SOMETIMES PEARY'S TEAM COULD BUILD A BRIDGE OF ICE TO CROSS A LEAD. OTHER TIMES, THEY HAD TO WAIT FOR THE WATER TO FREEZE SO THEY COULD MOVE AHEAD.

Sometimes they encountered real danger. They had to cross ice **floes** that could have broken off at any time, leaving them stranded and unable ever to get back on land. They once waited for almost a week to cross what they called the "Big **Lead,**" an area where water ran freely between ice floes.

On March 14, Peary sent two teams back to the *Roosevelt*. Henson led the rest forward. An hour later, he came to a small lead. He had to find a way to go around it. Their new route took them through snow so soft and deep that the sledges sunk. Henson wrote in his diary that the dogs became hard to handle. Sometimes they would do nothing, acting stubborn. Other times they acted wild and savage and fought fiercely with each other. Finally, the group got through this difficult section. But they faced another challenge right away. Just ahead, they found such jagged piles of ice that they had to get out their axes. Swinging the axes, they were able to hack away some ice. Then they could push it aside and clear a path.

On March 19, everybody made camp together. The next morning, Peary sent back assistant George Borup and his team of Inuit. The rest pushed on. On March 27, Peary decided it was time to thin the ranks again and sent back Ross Marvin and his team. On April 1, Robert Bartlett received orders to head back south. Bartlett was unhappy at first. He wanted to go on to the North Pole. But later he would admit that Henson was a better sledge driver and could help Peary more than he could.

There were just six people left in the expedition: Peary, Henson, and four Inuit. Finally, on April 6, Peary decided they had reached their goal. He planted the American flag and the group took photos. Now it was time to head home.

On the way back, the team raced along at what Henson called a "breakneck pace." Peary had become so tired that he could no longer walk. He rode on a sledge the entire way back. They were all miserable on the return, but Henson felt little fear. He enjoyed the sunlight, which was getting brighter every day.

On April 23, 1909, Peary's group finally set foot back on solid earth. They made it back to the *Roosevelt*. Henson said sad good-byes to Inuit friends. Never again would he return to the Arctic.

For the rest of his life, Peary would suffer from the injuries he had gotten in the Arctic. The expedition had been very difficult for him. In fact, Henson had saved Peary's life at least twice, first when Peary nearly drowned and later when a **musk ox** attacked him. Henson was in better health than Peary at the end of the trip. He went home with only an injured thumb and back pain. Still, he had lost 60 pounds during the expedition.

Back in the United States, newspapers carried long stories about the expedition and its success. At first, Peary did not receive the hero's welcome for which he had hoped. Another man, Frederick Cook, claimed that he had already reached the Pole. Eventually, scientists decided that Cook had lied. Peary went down in history as the first man to reach the North Pole.

In 1910, Peary wrote a book about the expedition to the North Pole. He took up a whole page listing awards and medals he had received. Henson never received such **acclaim.** Some newspaper stories mentioned him, but only in passing. If the general public did not take notice of Peary's most important assistant, African Americans did. Henson found that he was a source of great pride for African Americans. When he arrived home, he found thousands of telegrams and letters of congratulations waiting for him.

Courtesy of Verne Robinson

HENSON (CENTER) AND FOUR INUIT RAISED FIVE DIFFERENT FLAGS AT THE NORTH POLE. THE FLAGS REPRESENTED THE U.S. NAVY, PEARY'S COLLEGE FRATERNITY, THE NORTH POLE, THE DAUGHTERS OF THE AMERICAN REVOLUTION, AND THE RED CROSS.

ROBERT PEARY'S JOURNEY TO THE NORTH POLE MADE
HIM FAMOUS. HE RECEIVED AWARDS AND HONORS FOR THE
EXPEDITION. UNFORTUNATELY, FEW PEOPLE RECOGNIZED
THAT HENSON HAD HELPED TO MAKE THE TRIP POSSIBLE.

After the Pole

After Peary returned from the North Pole, he received recognition as a hero. He also became a rich man. Some of the awards he received included a cash prize. He made money selling his story to publishers and giving lectures.

Henson wrote his own book about his experiences called *A Negro Explorer at the North Pole,* which appeared in 1912. Soon after it appeared, the world forgot about him again. Never again would he live a life of such excitement.

For years, Matthew Henson's achievements went unnoticed. But when he was an old man, people took new interest in him. In 1937, the Explorers Club invited Henson to become a member. This club, which is still in operation today, was an **exclusive** group. It included only people who had undertaken serious voyages of exploration. This meant that other explorers voted to recognize Henson as an important explorer, too.

In 1945, like all the other American members of Peary's 1909 expedition, Henson received the U.S. Navy Medal. Unfortunately, because he was black, he was not invited to attend the ceremony where the others received their medals. In 1947, writer Bradley Robinson published a book called *Dark Companion*. He and Henson were good friends. Robinson based his biography on interviews and conversations with Henson. In 1954, thanks to efforts on the part of another, younger black Arctic explorer named Herbert Frisby, Henson received an invitation to go to the White House. There he met President Dwight D. Eisenhower.

On March 9, 1955, Henson died. He had reached the age of 88. In 1961, the state of Maryland placed a plaque in its state house in honor of Henson. It was the first southern state to so honor any black citizen.

In the 1980s, S. Allen Counter, a black professor of medicine at Harvard, became interested in Henson. He heard rumors that Henson had a grown son living in the Arctic. He traveled north to meet Henson's son by an Inuit woman. Counter eventually brought Henson's Inuit relatives to the United States to meet the rest of his family. They also visited his gravesite.

In 1988, Henson's coffin was dug up so that he could receive the honor of being buried at Arlington National Cemetery with other national heroes. In 1996, the U.S. Navy honored him by naming a ship after him, the USNS *Henson*. The ship is one of the navy's **survey** ships. This giant vessel is 329 feet long and is used to explore the ocean. It can house 55 people, including the 27 scientists who travel on the ship to study the world's oceans.

In recent years, some people questioned whether the Peary party actually reached the North Pole. The National Geographic Society wanted to know the truth, so they asked the Navigation Foundation for help. This group of experts studies the science of navigation.

The foundation's experts performed many calculations. They carefully studied the notes in Peary's diary. His records showed that he made the correct calculations. They looked at the angle of the sunlight in his photographs. Using a special method, they proved that the pictures were definitely taken at the North Pole. They performed other tests as well.

Finally, the Navigation Foundation determined that Peary and his team had, in fact, reached the Pole. *National Geographic* published this finding. The president of the National Geographic Society said, "Unless something better comes along, I consider this the end of a historic **controversy** and…due justice to a great explorer."

Most experts now believe that Peary and his team were the first to reach the Pole. On this great journey, Matthew Henson earned his own place in history. He is remembered not only as an assistant to Peary, but for his own amazing achievements during his years in the Arctic.

Library of Congress

MATTHEW HENSON SHOWS PRESIDENT EISENHOWER THE LOCATION OF THE NORTH POLE. IN 1954, EISENHOWER HONORED HENSON FOR HIS ACHIEVEMENTS IN THE ARCTIC.

Timeline

1866	Matthew Henson is born in Charles County, Maryland, on August 8.
1877	Henson runs away from home. He washes dishes at a restaurant in Washington, D.C., and lives with the restaurant's owner.
1878	Matthew goes to Baltimore. He becomes a cabin boy on a ship bound for China.
1884	Matthew gives up his life at sea following the death of his friend and employer, Captain Childs. Over the next four years, he holds several different jobs.
1887	As a clerk in a store in Washington, D.C., Henson waits on U.S. Navy officer Robert E. Peary. They strike up a conversation. Peary hires Henson as a valet to go along on an expedition to Nicaragua.
1891	Peary asks Henson to go with him on an expedition to Greenland.
1905	Peary and Henson try to reach the North Pole but fail.
1908	In the spring, Matthew Henson marries Lucy Jane Ross, his second wife.

1908	In July, Henson sails with Peary from New York City on a new expedition to the North Pole. They set up their winter camp in Canada two months later.
1909	The Peary expedition leaves their winter camp in Canada on March 1.
	On April 1, Peary and Henson, along with four Inuit, begin the last leg of their journey.
	On April 6, the team members reach the North Pole. They return to solid land on April 23.
1912	Matthew Henson's book, *A Negro Explorer at the North Pole*, is published.
1936	After more than 25 years of working in unskilled jobs, Henson finally retires at the age of 70.
1937	The Explorers Club elects Henson as a member.
1954	Henson is invited to the White House to meet President Eisenhower.
1955	Henson dies on March 9.
1988	Henson is reburied at Arlington National Cemetery.
1996	The U.S. Navy names a ship the USNS *Henson*, in honor of Matthew Henson's achievements.

Glossary

acclaim (uh-KLAYM)
Acclaim is high praise that people receive for something they have done. Henson received little acclaim for his role in Peary's expedition.

amendment (uh-MEND-ment)
An amendment is an addition or a change, including to the Constitution of the United States. The 13th Amendment abolished slavery.

American Civil War
(uh–MAYR–ih–kun SIV-el WAR)
The American Civil War was fought between the North and the South. It lasted from 1861 to 1865.

assistants (uh-SIS-tentz)
Assistants are helpers. Matthew Henson was Robert Peary's assistant.

cabin boy (KAB-in BOY)
A cabin boy was a servant on board a ship. Usually, a cabin boy took care of the needs of a ship's captain, such as doing his laundry and tidying up his cabin.

canal (kuh-NAL)
A canal is a waterway made by people. The Panama Canal was dug across Central America to let ships travel quickly from the Atlantic to the Pacific oceans.

controversy (KON-truh-vur-see)
A controversy is a dispute or argument. For many years, there was controversy about whether Peary and his team reached the North Pole.

engineer (en-jih-NEER)
An engineer is a person who designs, builds, and takes care of engines, machines, roads, and other things. Robert Peary was an engineer in the U.S. Navy.

exclusive (ek-SKLOO-siv)
If a club is exclusive, it is very selective about who it allows to become a member. The Explorers Club is an exclusive group of people who have taken part in important expeditions.

expedition (ek-spuh-DISH-un)
An expedition is a long journey made by one or more people for a special reason, such as reaching the North Pole. An explorer makes an expedition.

floes (FLOHZ)
Floes are fields or sheets of floating ice. The Peary team had to travel across floes.

frostbite (FRAWST-byt)
Frostbite is an injury to a body part caused by freezing. In the worst cases of frostbite, a person may need to have part of the body, such as a finger or toe, removed by surgery.

intrigued (in-TREEGD)
If people are intrigued by something, they are very interested or curious about it. Exploring the northern reaches of Greenland intrigued Peary.

Inuit (IN-yu-weht)
An Inuit is a member of the native groups who live in Greenland and the Arctic regions of Canada and Alaska. In the past, Americans called the Inuit "Eskimos."

Glossary

isthmus (IS-mus)
An isthmus is a narrow strip of land that connects two larger pieces of land. Nicaragua is part of the Central American isthmus, which connects North America to South America.

lead (LEED)
A lead is a split in the Arctic ice that exposes the water below. Crossing leads made travel in the Arctic difficult for the Peary team.

musk ox (MUSK OX)
A musk ox is a native animal of Greenland that looks like a woolly ox. Henson saved Peary's life when a musk ox attacked him.

narwhal (NAR-wahl)
A narwhal is a type of whale found in the Arctic waters. Henson hunted narwhal for food.

natives (NAY-tivz)
Natives of a place are people who were born there. The Inuit are natives who lived in the Arctic before explorers and settlers arrived.

navigator (nav-uh-GAY-tur)
A navigator is a person who keeps track of location and direction on a journey. Matthew Henson often acted as Peary's navigator.

pemmican (PEM-ih-ken)
Pemmican is a food made from a combination of dried meat and fat. Pemmican is very chewy.

porter (POR-tur)
A porter is a person employed to carry something heavy, such as another person's baggage. Matthew Henson worked as a porter.

recruited (ree-KREW-ted)
People are recruited when they are encouraged or invited to join a group. Robert Peary recruited assistants to join his polar expedition.

sextant (SEK-stent)
A sextant was a special scientific instrument. Years ago, sailors and explorers used a sextant to find out exactly where they are.

ship biscuit (SHIP BIS-kit)
Ship biscuit is a hard bread made of flour and water. Also called hardtack, it was carried on ships because it would last a long time.

sledges (SLEJ-ez)
Sledges are strong, heavy sleds. The Peary party traveled the Arctic on sledges pulled by dogs.

survey (sur-VAY)
When people survey something, they collect information to learn about it. The people aboard the USNS *Henson* survey the ocean.

valet (VAL-ay)
A valet is a servant who takes care of a man's clothes and provides other personal care. Matthew Henson was once Robert Peary's valet.

Index

African Americans
   freedom and, 12
   life in Philadelphia, 18
   poor treatment of, 14
   and Matthew Henson, pride in, 30
American Civil War, the, 12
Arctic
   characteristics of, 6, 21, 25
   difficulties of expedition to, 6, 9, 21, 22, 26, 29
   and sunlight, 25, 26, 29
   temperatures in, 25, 26
Arlington National Cemetery, 34

Central America, 17
Childs, Captain, 14, 15
Counter, S. Allen, 34
"Crane City," 26

Dark Companion, 33

Eisenhower, Dwight, 33, 35
Ellesmere Island, 6, 24, 25, 26
expeditions, supplies for, 6, 9, 18, 22, 25, 26
Explorers Club, 33

Frisby, Herbert, 33
frostbite, 9, 21

Greenland
   Peary expedition to, 14, 18, 21
   "problem," 14

Henson, Matthew
   birth of, 12
   book written by, 33
   children of, 34
   death of, 33
   and dog handling, 9, 22, 25
   and Explorer's Club, 33
   and Greenland expedition, 18
   honors received by, 33-34, 35
   injuries of, 21, 30
   and Inuit, 9, 20, 21, 22, 23, 30, 34
   lack of recognition and, 30, 32, 33
   marriage and, 18, 22, 25
   as navigator, 18
   and Peary, Robert, first meeting, 14, 16
   and reaching the North Pole, 7, 9-10
   skills of, 14, 18, 20, 21, 25
   and sledge building and repairing, 22, 25, 26, 27
   and sledge driving, 9, 21, 29
   travels of, 14, 15, 17

igloos, 9, 20, 22
Inuit, 6, 9. 20, 21, 22, 23, 25, 30
Isthmus of Panama, 17

lead, 28, 29

Maryland, 12, 14, 33

National Geographic, 34
Navigation Foundation, 34
A Negro Explorer at the North Pole, 33
Nicaragua, 17, 18
North Pole
   controversy and, 34
   first people to reach, 6, 9, 10, 11
   flags raised at, 31
   length of journey to, 26
   1905 expedition to, 22
   1909 expedition to, 6, 9-10, 11
   Peary expeditions to, map of, 19

Panama Canal, 17
Peary Arctic Club, 21
Peary, Josephine, 18, 21
Peary, Robert
   and controversy of North Pole expedition, 34
   dream of reaching the North Pole, 6, 21
   fame of, 30, 32, 33
   and Greenland, 14, 18, 21
   and Henson, Matthew,
   injuries of, 9, 29
   and Panama Canal, 17

Robinson, Bradley, 33
Roosevelt, the, 10, 24, 25, 26, 30
Roosevelt, Theodore, 25

sextant, 10
sledges, 6, 8, 9, 21, 26, 27, 29

13th Amendment, the, 12

USNS *Henson,* 34

Washington, D.C., 12

Further Information

Books

Goetzmann, William H., and Glyndwr Williams. *The Atlas of North American Exploration: From the Norse Voyages to the Race to the Pole.* New York: Prentice Hall, 1992.

Henson, Matthew A. *A Negro Explorer at the North Pole.* New York: Arno Press and the *New York Times,* 1969.

Rozakis, Laurie. *Matthew Henson and Robert Peary: The Race for the North Pole.* Woodbridge, CT: Blackbirch Press, 1994.

Bullen, Susan. *The Arctic and Its People.* Stamford, CT: Thompson Learning, 1994.

Magazine Articles

"The Henson Family," *National Geographic.* September 1988.

"New Evidence Places Peary at the Pole," *National Geographic.* January 1990.

Web Sites

Visit the Matthew Henson Memorial Web site:
http://www.matthewhenson.com

Read the biographies of Matthew Henson and Maryland's other famous African Americans at Maryland's African-American Heritage History Web site:
http://tqd.advanced.org/3337/main.html

Learn about an exciting solo expedition in the North Pole and explore the Arctic:
http://www.nationalgeographic.com/features/97/ice/

Learn about the Arctic life of the Inuit:
www.arctic-travel.com